BIG
CHEMISTRY
EXPERIMENTS
for little kids

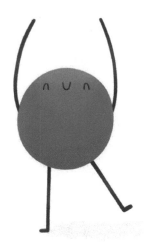

BIG CHEMISTRY EXPERIMENTS

for little kids

A First Science Book for Ages 3 to 5

Dr. Megan Olivia Hall, PhD, MAEd

Illustrations by Tanya Emelyanova

ROCKRIDGE
PRESS

For general information on our other products and services or to obtain technical support, please contact our Customer Care Department within the United States at (866) 744-2665, or outside the United States at (510) 253-0500.

Rockridge Press publishes its books in a variety of electronic and print formats. Some content that appears in print may not be available in electronic books, and vice versa.

TRADEMARKS: Rockridge Press and the Rockridge Press logo are trademarks or registered trademarks of Callisto Media Inc. and/or its affiliates, in the United States and other countries, and may not be used without written permission. All other trademarks are the property of their respective owners. Rockridge Press is not associated with any product or vendor mentioned in this book.

Series Designer: Heather Krakora
Interior and Cover Designer: Heather Krakora
Art Producer: Meg Baggott
Editor: Mary Colgan
Production Editor: Ruth Sakata Corley
Production Manager: Riley Hoffman

Illustrations © 2021 Tanya Emelyanova
Author photo courtesy of Rebecca Palmer

ISBN: Print 978-1-64876-108-9
eBook 978-1-64876-109-6
R0

For
Rosalea Brook Bickelhall,
my awesome daughter, and
Dylan Sky Bickelhall,
my fabulous son

CONTENTS

FOR THE ADULT SCIENTISTS

Kids ask a lot of questions about the world around them. The best way to answer them is with hands-on play and exploration whenever possible. That's where this book fits in. It is perfect for introducing your child to basic chemistry with simple experiments you can do at home.

The 20 experiments in this book illustrate chemistry principles like the density of different materials, chemical reactions, and the properties of air and water. Each experiment has simple instructions, an approximate time allotment, questions to ask your child to get them to think about what they see, and easy-to-understand explanations of the science behind the activities.

It's important for adults to allow kids to be part of every step of their experiments, including setup and cleanup. When you see this symbol, ⚠ , it means kids will need a little extra help and supervision from an adult for one or more steps.

Science can be messy. Each experiment has a handy "Messy Meter" with a rating from 1 to 5. The higher the number, the messier the experiment will be. Remember to always protect the working area and have your little scientist wear old clothes or a smock.

As you experiment together, don't worry about what is supposed to happen or if you're doing everything perfectly. When you are surprised, curious, and inventive, you're modeling scientific ways of thinking for your child. When you have fun with these chemistry labs, you will show your child just how awesome this journey can be!

KID SCIENTIST!

Do you have questions about the world around you? Do you want to know what's inside clouds, why things sink or float, and what happens when you mix chemicals together? If so, then it sounds like you are ready to become a scientist!

The world is full of stuff you can see, smell, taste, touch, and hear. Scientists call this stuff *matter*. Chemistry is a kind of science that explores all of the different types of matter in the world.

This book is full of fun chemistry experiments for you to try. Real scientists use the scientific method when they experiment. You can use it, too, when you do the activities in this book!

The Scientific Method

1. Ask a question.

2. Make a guess.

3. Do an experiment.

4. Gather information.

5. Tell other people what you discovered.

Are you ready to experiment? Put on your lab coat and let's go!

MESSY METER

Golden Treasure Bubbles

Experiment time: 15 minutes

What happens when you try to mix oil and water?

WHAT YOU NEED

Pint-size jar or bottle
with lid

Water

Orange gel food
coloring

Vegetable oil

Fill the jar ¾ full
with water.

Add 5 to 10 drops of food
coloring. Stop when the
water is bright orange.

Pour vegetable oil into the jar
until it is full.

Firmly attach the lid to the jar. Shake well until everything mixes together.

Set the jar down and watch what happens!

BE CURIOUS

Why do you think this experiment is called Golden Treasure Bubbles? Where are the oil and water before you shake the jar? How do they change when you shake the jar? After you set the jar down, what happens?

HOW IT WORKS

When you shake oil and water together, they don't mix. Instead, the two liquids break up into many small droplets. When the shaking stops, the droplets of each liquid join back together. They go back to one big layer of water and a smaller layer of oil. The oil floats on top of the water because oil is lighter than water.

MESSY METER

Play Dough Play

Experiment time: 30 minutes

How do ingredients turn into play dough?

WHAT YOU NEED

Small mixing bowl (needs to hold about 2 cups)

1 cup flour

¼ cup salt

1 tablespoon cream of tartar

Small cup (needs to hold about ⅔ cup)

Mixing spoon

Gel food coloring

½ cup warm water

1 tablespoon cooking oil

In a bowl, mix the flour, salt, and cream of tartar.

Stir 3 drops of food coloring into the warm water.

Add the oil to the colored water.

Pour the water and oil into the flour mixture.

Mix everything together with your hands until it forms into dough.

Take your play dough out of the bowl and get ready to play!

What happened when you added oil to the colored water? How did the play dough change as you mixed it? What would happen if you played with the dough while it was still wet and sticky?

HOW IT WORKS

A mixture is a material that is made up of things that can be separated. A bowl of cereal with milk is a mixture; you can separate the pieces of cereal from the milk. The flour, salt, and cream of tartar make a mixture in this experiment. When you mixed those with the wet ingredients, they stopped being separate and made something brand-new: play dough!

MESSY METER

Water Power

Experiment time: 15 minutes

Do things float better on plain water or soapy water?

WHAT YOU NEED

2 small mixing bowls or
regular table bowls

Water

Mixing spoon

Dish soap

2 squares of wax paper cut
to fit just inside each bowl

Pennies

1

Fill one bowl with water. Set it aside.

2

Fill the other bowl with water. Stir in a drop or two of dish soap.

3

Gently place a piece of wax paper on the water's surface in each bowl.

WAX PAPER

4

In the bowl of plain water, gently place pennies, one at a time, on the wax paper until they sink.

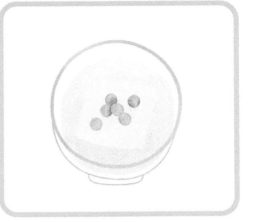

5

In the bowl of soapy water, gently place pennies, one at a time, on the wax paper until they sink.

6

Place the bowls side by side. What do you notice?

BE CURIOUS

How many pennies were able to sit on the plain water before sinking? How many were able to sit on the soapy water? What do you think might happen if you added more soap?

HOW IT WORKS

Water sticks to itself to form a thin "skin" on its surface. This is called surface tension. Surface tension gives water the power to hold things up that wouldn't usually float. When you add soap to water, the soap takes away the water's surface tension. This is why things can't float as well on soapy water.

MESSY METER

Dye Your Socks

Experiment time: 30 minutes

How can you make dye brighter?

1 pair children's white
cotton socks

2 bowls (1 small and
1 medium)

Vinegar

Warm water

1 tablespoon
turmeric

Place one sock in the small bowl and cover it with vinegar. Soak for 10 minutes.

Fill the medium bowl with warm water and mix in the turmeric.

Take the sock out of the vinegar and wring it out.

Place both socks—one wet and one dry—into the bowl of turmeric water for 10 minutes.

Take the socks out of the bowl and wring them out. Rinse the socks with water, and then dry them in a dryer.

Place the socks on a table (or on your feet!). Do you see a difference?

BE CURIOUS

What happened to the socks when you added them to the turmeric mixture? At the end of the experiment, did the sock that had been soaked in vinegar look different from the sock that was dry?

HOW IT WORKS

Dye, like yellow turmeric, is a kind of matter that sticks to other matter. When dye touches cotton, it sticks to the white cotton and changes its color. Vinegar helps the dye stick to the cotton better. This makes the color brighter. Cotton is white when it is growing on its plant. It turns color only when mixed with dyes.

MESSY METER

Rain Cloud in a Cup

Experiment time: 20 minutes

Why does rain fall from clouds?

WHAT YOU NEED

Tall clear glass

Water

Foam shaving cream

Small cup

Blue gel food coloring

Pipette or dropper

Fill the tall glass about ¾ full with water.

Squirt shaving cream on top of the water to make a "cloud."

In a small cup, mix ¼ cup of water and 3 drops of food coloring. This will be the "rain."

Use the pipette to drip the colored water onto your cloud until it starts to "rain" into the water.

Watch it rain!

Did the rain stay on top of the cloud? Where did it go? What happened when the rain reached the water?

HOW IT WORKS

As you dripped colored water on top of your shaving cream, it made your cloud heavier and heavier. When the water got too heavy for the cloud, it sank through and "rained" into the glass. Clouds in the sky are made of tiny water droplets. When the droplets get heavy enough, they sink through the clouds and fall as rain.

MESSY METER

Candy Rainbows

Experiment time: 15 minutes

Do M&M's dissolve differently in warm and cold water?

Two white plates

M&M's candy

Warm water

Cold water

1

Make a pattern on one of the plates with some of the M&M's.

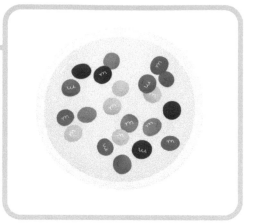

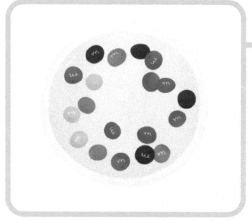

2

On the other plate, use more M&M's to make a similar pattern.

3

Slowly pour warm water onto one plate until all of the candies are covered.

4

Slowly pour cold water onto the other plate until all of the candies are covered.

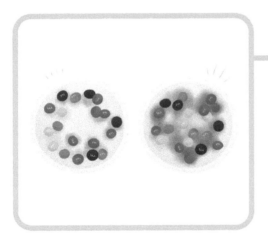

5

Set the plates side by side and watch the colors swirl.

BE CURIOUS

What happened when the water covered the candies? Was there a difference between the warm water and cold water? What might happen if you used warmer water? What about ice water?

HOW IT WORKS

The colorful coating on M&M's is made from chemicals that mix easily with water. When you poured water over the candies, the chemicals dissolved. This means the chemicals became part of the water. Warm water is better at dissolving chemicals than cold water, so it pulled off the candies' colors faster.

MESSY METER

Icy Hot

Experiment time: 15 minutes (plus freezing time)

Does hot or cold water sink?

WHAT YOU NEED

Ice cube tray

Water for ice cubes

Red and blue food coloring

Large clear bowl

Room temperature water

Small cup

4 tablespoons hot water

Fill an ice cube tray with water. Add 3 drops of blue food coloring to each cube and mix. Freeze overnight.

Fill a large clear bowl ¾ full with room temperature water.

In a small cup, mix 12 drops of red food coloring with 4 tablespoons of hot water.

Place a blue ice cube in the water on one side of the bowl.

Slowly pour the hot red water into the water on the other side of the bowl.

Watch how the colors move!

BE CURIOUS

What happened to the ice cube when you put it in the bowl? Where did the red water go after you poured it into the bowl? Did the colors mix? Let the bowl sit for an hour. Does it look the same?

HOW IT WORKS

Hot water rises, and cold water sinks. This is because hot water is less dense, or lighter, than cold water. In this experiment, the warm red water floated on the room temperature water, while the cold water from the ice cube sunk to the bottom of the bowl. Once all the water became the same temperature, the colors could mix.

MESSY METER

Marshmallow Puffball

Experiment time: 15 minutes

What happens when air gets hot?

WHAT YOU NEED

2 marshmallows

Edible ink pens

2 microwave-safe plates

Microwave

Draw a face on each marshmallow with an edible ink
pen (or a toothpick and
food coloring).

Place one marshmallow
on a plate. Microwave for
20 seconds.

Remove the marshmallow
from the microwave. Com-
pare it to the uncooked
marshmallow.

4 ⚠

Place the second marshmallow on the second plate. Microwave for 40 seconds.

5

Place the two marshmallows side by side.

BE CURIOUS

How did the two marshmallows change? Did both marshmallows puff up to the same size? Did the marshmallows go back to their original shape after they cooled down? Did they feel different after they cooled?

HOW IT WORKS

Hot air takes up more space than cool air. Marshmallows are mostly made of tiny air bubbles. A microwaved marshmallow puffs up because the hot air in the bubbles expands, or gets bigger. When you take the marshmallow out of the microwave, the air bubbles inside cool down and get smaller.

MESSY METER

Paint on Ice

Experiment time: 25 minutes (plus freezing time)

What happens when you paint on frozen ice and melting ice?

WHAT YOU NEED

Baking sheet

Water

Water-based paints

Paintbrush

2 sheets of white paper

Fill a baking sheet with water and freeze it overnight.

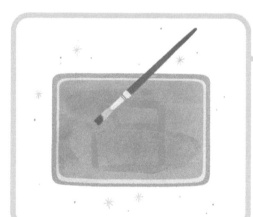

Paint a picture on the ice right after it comes out of the freezer.

Lightly press a piece of paper onto the ice painting, and then peel it off.

4

Bring the ice to the sink and rinse with water. Let the excess water drip off.

5

Paint another picture on the surface of the wet ice.

6

Lightly press a piece of paper onto the ice painting, and then peel it off.

7 →

7

Put your paintings on a table to dry, and then show them off!

BE CURIOUS

When you pulled the papers off the ice, you had prints of your ice paintings. What things about your prints were the same? What things were different?

HOW IT WORKS

Ice is frozen water. Ice is so hard that it can't mix with paint. Painting on ice is like painting on paper. When ice melts, it turns into water again. When the ice got wet, it started to melt. The water mixed with the paint and didn't hold its shape as well.

MESSY METER

Invisible Ink

Experiment time: 20 minutes

How does grape juice make invisible ink appear?

2 small cups

Mixing spoon

1 tablespoon
baking soda

1 tablespoon water

Paintbrush

Sheet of white paper

Purple grape juice

Pipette or dropper

1

In one of the cups, use a spoon to stir together the baking soda and water.

2

Dip the paintbrush into the mixture and use it to paint on the paper. Set the paper aside to dry.

3

After your painting dries, pour some grape juice into the other cup, and then use the pipette to drip purple grape juice on the paper where you painted.

4

Enjoy your drawing!

BE CURIOUS

Did your painting stay invisible after you dripped grape juice on it? What color is the grape juice? What color are the lines of your painting? What do you think would happen if you dripped red fruit punch on your painting?

HOW IT WORKS

A fruit juice's color comes from chemicals. Grape juice contains a special purple chemical. When grape juice mixes with the drawing you made with baking soda, the purple chemical changes into a brand-new chemical. The new chemical isn't purple—it's blue! Scientists call this a chemical reaction.

MESSY METER

Exploding Foam

Experiment time: 25 minutes

What happens when you make a lot of bubbles all at once?

WHAT YOU NEED

Empty (12- to 16-ounce) plastic bottle

3% hydrogen peroxide

Liquid dish soap

Food coloring

Small cup

¼ cup warm water

1 (¼-ounce) packet dry yeast (about 2¼ teaspoons)

Mixing spoon

Fill the plastic bottle ⅓ full of hydrogen peroxide and set it inside a sink.

Add one big squirt of liquid dish soap to the bottle.

Add 5 drops of food coloring to the bottle.

Pour the warm water into a small cup. Add the yeast and stir with a spoon for 1 minute.

Pour the yeast mixture into the bottle.

Watch what happens!

BE CURIOUS

What happened when you poured the yeast mixture into the bottle? What came out of the bottle? What do you think made the bubbles? Touch the jar. Is it warm or cold?

HOW IT WORKS

Yeast is a living creature. Living creatures can make chemical reactions happen. One kind of chemical reaction breaks apart substances like hydrogen peroxide. The yeast made oxygen bubbles as it broke apart the hydrogen peroxide. This reaction caused heat. The soap trapped the bubbles and made foam.

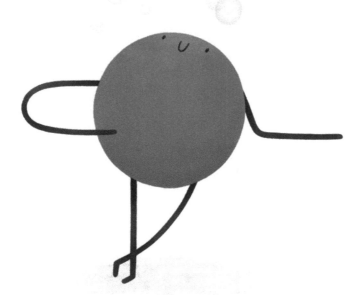

MESSY METER

Play Dough Volcano

Experiment time: 30 minutes

What happens when baking soda mixes with vinegar?

WHAT YOU NEED

Play dough (see page 5 to make your own)

Empty (12- to 16-ounce) plastic bottle

Funnel

1 cup vinegar

Orange food coloring

Dish soap

½ cup baking soda

1

Use play dough to make a volcano shape around your empty bottle.

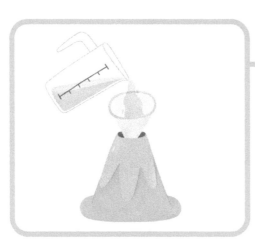

2

Place your volcano in the sink. Use the funnel to pour the vinegar into the bottle.

3

Add 4 drops of food coloring to the bottle.

Add a couple squirts of dish soap to the bottle.

Use the funnel to add the baking soda to the volcano.

Stand back and watch the "lava" flow!

BE CURIOUS

Why do you think we used orange food coloring for this experiment? Why do you think the lava was bubbly? What would happen if you used more vinegar and baking soda?

HOW IT WORKS

When baking soda and vinegar mix, they turn into different chemicals. One of these chemicals is a gas called carbon dioxide. Gases take up a lot of space. You made so much gas, it exploded out of the top of the bottle!

MESSY METER

Shiny Pennies

Experiment time: 10 minutes

What happens when you soak pennies in salty vinegar?

2 regular table bowls

¼ cup water

¼ cup vinegar

Mixing spoon

1 teaspoon salt

6 dull old pennies

Paper towels

1

Fill one bowl with the water and the other bowl with the vinegar.

2

Using a spoon, stir the salt into the vinegar.

3

Place three pennies into the salty vinegar mixture and the other three pennies into the water.

4 Watch all six pennies for 1 to 3 minutes. Note what happens.

5 Take the pennies out of the bowls and place them on a paper towel.

BE CURIOUS

What happened to the pennies in the salty vinegar? Did this happen to the pennies that you soaked in water?

HOW IT WORKS

Air makes shiny new pennies look dull and dirty over time. When you mix salt and vinegar together, you make a chemical that can clean off this dull coating. If you don't rinse the salty vinegar off your pennies and let them sit for a while, a chemical reaction will turn your pennies green!

MESSY METER

Soda Fountain

Experiment time: 20 minutes

What happens when Mentos candy mixes with diet soda?

WHAT YOU NEED

2 index cards

Clear tape

1 (12-ounce or 2-liter)
plastic bottle of diet Coke
or diet Pepsi

Mentos candies (4 for a
12-ounce bottle of soda;
12 for a 2-liter bottle)

1 Make one index card into a tube by rolling and taping it. It should be just wide enough to fit the Mentos.

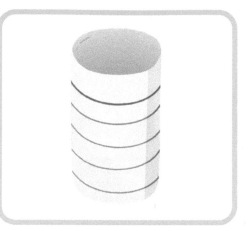

2 Place the soda bottle on the ground OUTSIDE and take off the cap.

3 Place the other index card flat over the open soda bottle top.

4

Place your tube on the index card directly over the bottle top. Hold the tube in place as you fill it with Mentos.

5

While holding the tube, quickly pull the flat index card away so the Mentos fall into the open bottle.

6

Stand WAY back and watch how high your fountain sprays!

How quickly did something happen? How high was your soda fountain? Did the explosion use up the soda? Were there any Mentos left in the bottle?

HOW IT WORKS

Soda is made of gas bubbles, water, sugar, and flavor. The gas bubbles usually come out of the soda slowly because the water traps them inside. Mentos help the bubbles come out really quickly. Most of the soda is still left over, but you might not be able to tell if your fountain shot soda out with the bubbles.

MESSY METER

Slippery Slime

Experiment time: 25 minutes

How can you turn glue into slime?

1 (3- or 4-ounce) bottle of plain white glue (such as Elmer's)

Disposable table bowl

Food coloring, any color

Disposable mixing spoon

2 teaspoons baking soda

2 tablespoons contact lens solution containing boric acid, plus more if needed

1

Pour the entire bottle of glue into the bowl.

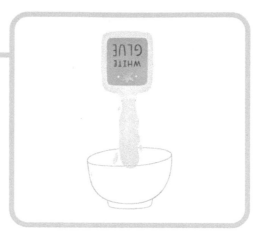

2

Add 10 drops of food coloring and stir well with a spoon.

3

Add the baking soda to the glue mixture.

Add the contact lens solution to the mixture.

Stir the mixture until a ball of slime forms. Add more contact lens solution if the slime is too sticky.

Take your slime out of the bowl and get ready to stretch and pull.

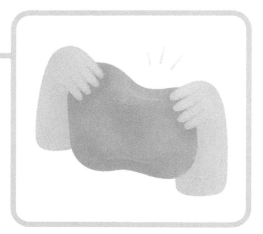

BE CURIOUS

How does the slime feel? How is slime different from glue? Which materials in your glue mixture do you think changed the glue into slime?

HOW IT WORKS

Glue is made of long strands of a special material that slide past each other, sort of like wet hair. Contact lens solution makes these strands stick together. This chemical reaction turns the liquid glue into the gooey and stretchy slime you love!

MESSY METER

Cinnamon Burst

Experiment time: 5 minutes

Which flavors do you sense with your tongue?
Which flavors do you sense with your nose?

· · · · · · · **WHAT YOU NEED** · · · · · ·

1 spicy, chewy cinnamon
candy (such as Hot Tamales)

Take a deep breath in.

Gently pinch your
nose closed.

Put a candy in your mouth
and chew it three times without breathing in.

4

Let go of your nose and take a deep breath in.

BE CURIOUS

What did you taste while your nose was pinched shut? What did you taste when you let go of your nose?

HOW IT WORKS

Your tongue can taste five flavors: sweet, salty, sour, bitter, and umami (also called savory). You also "taste" all other flavors with your nose. When your nose was closed, you could taste only the sweet sugar in the candy. When your nose was open, you could smell (and taste) the strong cinnamon flavor in the candy. What a surprise!

MESSY METER

Inky Potatoes

Experiment time: 20 minutes

What happens when iodine mixes with potato starch?

Paintbrush

Iodine (Betadine or povidone-iodine will work)

1 potato, sliced

1

Dip a paintbrush into the iodine.

2

Lightly brush a thin layer of iodine all over the potato slices, including the edges.

3

Check on the slices every minute for 10 minutes. What do you notice?

BE CURIOUS

What color was the iodine when you first put it on the potato slices? How did the color of the iodine change? Are the painted potato slices the same color all over? What do you think would happen if you put more iodine on the potato slices?

HOW IT WORKS

Iodine is a brown chemical that turns blue, purple, or black when it mixes with a chemical called starch. Potatoes have a lot of starch in them, especially around their edges. Different parts of the potato have different amounts of starch. Iodine might turn darker colors in the places where there is more starch.

MESSY METER

Filtering Water

Experiment time: 20 minutes

When a mixture moves through a filter, what does it leave behind?

WHAT YOU NEED

Funnel

Clear cup

Shredded paper

Play sand

Coffee grounds

Drinking cup filled with water

Mixing spoon

69

Place a funnel in a clear cup.

Starting with shredded paper, make several layers of play sand and shredded paper inside the funnel.

Mix a large spoonful of coffee grounds into a cup of water.

4

Slowly pour your coffee mixture into the funnel.

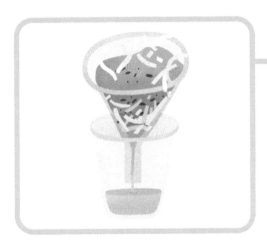

5

Watch the filtered water drip into the cup. (This water is not for drinking!)

BE CURIOUS

Did the water look or smell different before and after it went through the funnel? Did the sand or shredded paper look different after the water went through them? What was left behind?

HOW IT WORKS

You built a filter. When you poured your coffee ground mixture into the funnel filter, the coffee grounds got stuck while the water flowed through. The water in the cup was cleaner than it was before you poured it into the funnel. In nature, sand and soil filter rainwater the same way.

MESSY METER

Fizzy Seashells

Experiment time: 15 minutes

What happens to seashells in vinegar?

2 seashells

2 clear cups

Vinegar

Water

Place one seashell
in each cup.

Pour the vinegar into one cup
until the seashell is covered.

Pour the water into the
other cup until the seashell
is covered.

Check on both cups every minute for 10 minutes.

BE CURIOUS

What did you notice happening in one of the cups? Were bubbles coming from the seashell in the cup with vinegar or water? What do you think might happen if you left the seashell in vinegar overnight or for many days?

HOW IT WORKS

Seashells are made of a chemical that reacts with vinegar. When a seashell is put in vinegar, it begins to break down and forms gas bubbles. If the shell stays in the vinegar long enough, it will fall apart. We need to keep chemicals like vinegar out of our oceans to help protect the animals that live inside seashells.

MESSY METER

Salty Seeds

Experiment time: 15 minutes to set up, plus several days for seeds to sprout

Does salt change the way that seeds sprout?

WHAT YOU NEED

2 paper towels

2 snack-size zip-top bags

Water

½ teaspoon salt

Unpopped popcorn

Masking tape

Fold both paper towels and place one inside each zip-top bag.

Pour enough water into each bag to soak the paper towel. Then add 1 to 2 tablespoons more.

Sprinkle the salt into one of the bags.

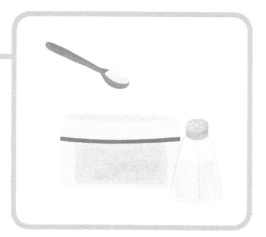

4

Place seven popcorn seeds in each bag between the bag and the wet paper towel. Seal the bags.

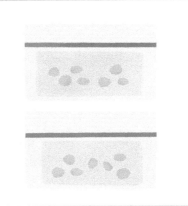

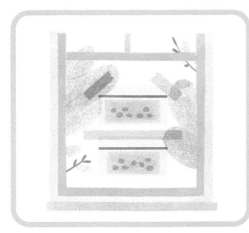

5

Tape the bags to a window so you can see the seeds indoors.

6

Check on the bags daily for one week to watch your seeds sprout.

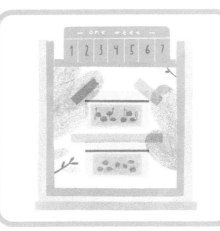

BE CURIOUS

Did more popcorn seeds sprout in the bag with salt or without salt? What do you think would happen if you used half the amount of salt?

HOW IT WORKS

Seeds need water to sprout. Salt absorbs water. Salt stops seeds from sprouting by drying them out.

ABOUT THE AUTHOR

Dr. Megan Olivia Hall, PhD, MAEd, is the 2013 Minnesota Teacher of the Year. As a science teacher, Megan has worked with learners of many ages and levels, from kindergarteners to graduate students. A National Board Certified Teacher, she serves as science department chair and develops anti-racist social-emotional curricula at Open World Learning Community in Saint Paul Public Schools. Megan's writing has been featured in *Education Week* and *The Science Teacher*. She is the author of *Awesome Kitchen Science Experiments for Kids*. A Leading Educator Ambassador for Equity Fellow with the Education Civil Rights Alliance, Megan holds a PhD in Learning, Instruction, and Innovation from Walden University.

ABOUT THE ILLUSTRATOR

Tanya Emelyanova was born in Siberia, where she studied advertising and mass communication. But since drawing has always been her true passion, she embarked on an illustration and pattern design career. Now she is working from her home studio in Saint Petersburg. Tanya loves to create cute and funny characters and illustrations for children's books and magazines, printed art, and more, combining both digital and analog materials.

Printed in the USA
CPSIA information can be obtained
at www.ICGtesting.com
CBHW041957070724
11047CB00002B/5